RAMBLINGS OF AN OLD GUY
(And a couple of his friends)

A collection of poems
about life, love,
and "other stuff"

By Randall L. Boyd

Text Copyright ©2016 Randall L. Boyd

Original Copyright 2016 Randall L. Boyd

Publishing Copyright ©2016 Laurel Rose Publishing

Laurel Rose Publishing

www.laurelrosepublishing.com

laurelrosepublishing@gmail.com

ISBN-10: 1-944583-07-6
ISBN-13: 978-1-944583-07-1

No part of this book may be reproduced, stored in a retrieval system, or transmitted by any means without the written permission of the author.

Ramblings of an Old Guy — Randall L. Boyd

TABLE OF CONTENTS

PREFACE 6
Endorsements 7
INTRODUCTION 8
I CAN'T QUIT NOW! 9
A 737, A STORM, AND A BRUSH WITH ETERNITY 10
POSITIVE THOUGHTS 14
A FRIENDSHIP LOST 15
REBELLION 16
A PROMISE BROKEN 17
BAGGAGE LOST 18
REFLECTING ON THE PAST 19
COMINGS & GOINGS 21
SHE IS STRENGTH 22
CHRISTIE TAYLOR DUSCHEL 23
IF I CAN FIND THE TIME 24
CHANGE DIRECTION 25
TRAVELING THE ROAD OF TIME 26
WHY DID I FIGHT SO HARD? 27
THE LIE 28
THE CROWD CHOOSES 29
FEELING STUCK IN THE MIDDLE 30
DAUGHTERS 31
THE BATTLE 32
SHE'S GOT THIS 33
WILL YOU BITE THE HAND THAT FEEDS? 35

Ramblings of an Old Guy — Randall L. Boyd

FAILURE	36
REGRETS	37
TALKS WITH GRANDMA	38
FORGIVENESS IS NOT EASY	39
THE NEVER ENDING CYCLE	40
SPRING	40
SUMMER	41
AUTUMN	42
WINTER	43
HAPPINESS	44
HOLDING UP TRAFFIC ON THE FREEWAY	45
THE BOX	47
WE MUST NOT FAIL	48
TALL AND BEAUTIFUL	49
I DON'T MISS YOU NOW	50
TO THE FOOL WHO THREW HER AWAY	51
JUNK, JUNK	52
I STAND ALONE	54
MOM'S KITCHEN	56
TIRED	57
SITTING IN DARKNESS	58
MELISSA COOK	59
PURPLE	60
DRAWING A BLANK	61
PARENTING	62
FEELING LONELY, FOOLISH, AND USED	63

Ramblings of an Old Guy — Randall L. Boyd

PEONIES	65
MY SAFE ROOM	67
REALITY	68
THOUGHTS LOCKED AWAY	70
THE IMPORTANT GIFTS	71
DECAY	72
NOW HE KNOWS HOW TO WIN	74
DISTURBED	77
ON BEING A FOSTER PARENT	78
CONFUSED	79
BLESSINGS ON YOU ALL	80
About the Author	81

PREFACE

This book is dedicated, first and foremost, to my Lord and Creator, who instilled in me from the beginning an appreciation for the written word, and from whom I received the talent to write poetry.

Special thanks to my wife, Jimmie, who is my inspiration, for putting up with all the times I was up at all hours of the night working on this project. You are my rock. I do not know what I would do without you.

To my children, John, Andrea, Michelle, Melissa, and Reannon... You are my pride, my joy, my legacy. Words cannot express what you mean to me. It is an honor and a privilege to be your dad.

To my grandchildren Isaak, Harley, Wesley, Levi, Ella, Parker, Ryan, and Rachel, of whom I am most proud... I am awed at your accomplishments thus far in life. God has blessed me so richly, so much more than I deserve!
You are my life.

Finally, to an old and dear friend, the late Jo Nell Fulwiler, a friend since high school, and a published author, who also loved and wrote poetry... You encouraged me to continue to write many years ago when I was frustrated and ready to quit. You told me my poetry was worthy of publication. Thank you. If not for you, this book might never have been written.

Endorsements

Bro. Boyd,

Thank you for sharing these personal poems. I can tell they are beautifully, creatively written from the heart! They show the extent of emotions, passion, and life in general. You have a wonderful gift that I trust you will continue to use.

The poem entitled "A 737, a Storm, and a Brush with Eternity" was an amazing poetic, real-life story. And since I love the color Purple, Melissa Cook's poem entitled the same was beautiful. There were several more that jumped out at me, and needless to say it's a great read.

I especially like the two guest authors you used as well. There is a wonderful dynamic symmetry between mentoring, collaboration and expression.

Thank you again for sharing. It is wonderful!

Blessings,

Aaron Batchelor   Pastor, New Life Center

Randy;

I have read your book. Delightful! I laughed, cried, felt anger and delight. God has surely gifted you to write.

Blessings

Garry Tracy

INTRODUCTION

I began writing poetry when I was in Junior High School, way back in ancient times. At the time, it was just an assignment, and I dreaded it. Our class was assigned to write three original poems, and to select three additional poems that we liked, from any book in the library, and write a paper describing what we liked about each. However, as the assignment progressed, I discovered that I actually liked several different types of poetry. I ended up enjoying that assignment. My teacher, unfortunately, was not nearly as impressed with my poems as I was. Be that as it may, I was hooked, and I have been writing poetry ever since.

This book is a collection of poems about life, love, and "other stuff." Each of the poems I chose to include in this book, with one exception, are written about things or situations I have either experienced personally, or were inspired by things others close to me experienced. It is my hope that those who read this book can identify with some or all of the subject matter, and the feelings and emotions I have tried to express.

In addition, I have included several poems written by two guest authors. These two individuals are very special to me, and are each very, very talented. I will say no more about them here. You will find a brief bio about each of them included with their poems.

With that said, we hope you enjoy reading this book as much as we enjoyed writing it and putting it all together.

Ramblings of an Old Guy — Randall L. Boyd

I CAN'T QUIT NOW!

I once thought I was invincible,
that nothing could ever stop me.
I once thought I was king of the world,
and nobody could ever top me.
I once thought I was immortal,
that I would live forever.
I thought I had it all figured out,
I was bright, and smart, and clever.
And now I find those thoughts of mine
are growing rather cold.
No matter how hard I resist, my friends,
I'm really getting old.
No longer am I invincible,
I'm smarter than that now.
I will never be king of the world,
I figured that out somehow.
Immortality has eluded me,
there's nothing I can do.
All the things I had figured out,
I mostly figured wrong, too.
When I look back upon my youth,
the mistakes of my past,
It's hard for me to understand
how I made it this far, this fast.
But I'm not finished yet, my friend,
I have more races to run.
No, I can't quit running now,
'cause I'm still havin' fun!

Randall L. Boyd, August 1, 2003

Ramblings of an Old Guy   Randall L. Boyd

A brief word, if I may, before you read this one. The events I am attempting to describe in this poem are true. I was aboard this flight. The fear was real. Our pilots did an amazing, extraordinary job landing the plane in some of the worst conditions imaginable. I have been told I should have written this as an essay instead of a poem. Perhaps so, but I am a poet, so what you see is what you get.

A 737, A STORM, AND A BRUSH WITH ETERNITY

Love Field in Dallas,
weather is clear.
A beautiful fall night in Texas.
Southwest is on time tonight, as usual.
An almost perfect
"ten minute turnaround"
and we are under way.
We taxi to the runway.
We wait.
What are we waiting for?
We wait.
We are beginning to taxi again.
In the other direction.
Why?
Pilot tells us the wind has shifted.
We must take off from the other end.
OK. Let's go.
I want to get home.
Finally, airborne! Smooth flight.

I must have dozed off.
What was that?
I'm awake now, for sure!
Lightning.

Ramblings of an Old Guy   Randall L. Boyd

Thunder.
Driving rain.
Wind tossing a Boeing 737
around like a toy.
Pilot says we are on final approach to Little Rock.

Fasten seat belts.
Expect turbulence.
No kidding.
Wind shear...
We are dropping much too fast.
Pilots rev engines and abort the approach.

Tossed around like a rag doll
in a bulldog's mouth.
I am worried.
In thousands of miles flown,
I have never experienced anything
close to this.
Flight attendants finding seats.
Strapping themselves in.
They are worried.
I can tell by the way they look at each other.
Nobody is speaking.
A little girl begins to cry.

A second approach at Little Rock.
Strong wind.
Tossed back and forth.
Pilots are struggling to maintain control.
I can tell by the tone of his voice.
"Ladies and gentlemen,
normally we would divert due to the weather.
Unfortunately, we do not have that much fuel left.
We must land here in Little Rock.
Don't worry,

Ramblings of an Old Guy   Randall L. Boyd

we're gonna land safely soon.
Please stay in your seats.
Do not get up for any reason.
Everything is fine."
Lightning, Thunder, Strong Wind.
Pilots abort our second approach.
Several people are crying now.
Some praying.

A man across from me begins to curse.
Pilots begin third approach.
Violent turbulence.
Jerking, up, down, left, right.
Lightning is green.
I have never seen green lightning.
We are nearing the runway.
We touch down.
On one wheel, the left one.
Plane is tilted to the left.
Time seems to stand still.
The right wheel finally touches down.
I've landed here a thousand times.
We are using too much runway.
Just beyond the end of the runway
is the Arkansas River.
Pilots know it, too.
Too late to abort our landing now.
Nose wheel still not down.
Pilot brakes hard.
Nose wheel slams down.
Pilot revs engines, reversing thrust
Trying to slow the plane down.

The plane stops.
Finally.
We are at the end of the runway.

Ramblings of an Old Guy — Randall L. Boyd

No room to spare.
No runway left.
Plane sitting dead still.
We begin to taxi to the terminal.
Plane is still being shaken by the wind.
Passengers crying
and clapping at the same time.
All of us know just how close we came
to eternity that stormy October night.

Exiting the plane.
Pilots emerge from cockpit,
visibly shaken, but relieved.
We shake their hands,
we say thank you.
One pilot and I have shaken hands
many times before.
I usually say, "Good job," or "Smooth flight,"
But tonight my words are more sincere,
"Thank you.
That was a great landing."
He smiles and says,
"You're welcome."
Then he winks and says, "I hope
Southwest doesn't expect us
To leave here anytime soon tonight!"
He smiles, I smile,
I go my way, he goes his.
But he will have my never ending gratitude
for getting that bird
on the ground in one piece
that awful October night.

Randy Boyd, October, 1985

POSITIVE THOUGHTS

Positive thoughts make a difference.
It doesn't mean bad situations will not come,
But a positive attitude does seem to
Make them easier to deal with.
So instead of complaining,
Try being thankful.
Instead of crying, laugh.
Instead of dwelling on problems, do something.
Instead of frowning, smile.
Live life to the fullest.
Love without strings attached.
Positive attitude
Plus positive thoughts
Equals a positive life,
Which equals a happy life.
So think positive.

Randall L. Boyd, June 1, 2016

A FRIENDSHIP LOST

We were once friends,
Good friends,
Or so I thought.
We visited often.
We were there for each other
In good times and bad.
We were friends.
Things change, people change.
One day things did change.
I had to move away.
We said we'd stay friends.
We vowed to stay in touch.
We said we would talk often.
We did.
For a while.
But then responses
Came less and less often.
As time traveled on
My friend became distant.
Then he stopped corresponding at all.
Sad.
Our friendship was important,
At least to me.
I valued it.
I treasured it.
Maybe… Maybe one day
We can be friends again.
I hope.

-Randy Boyd, March, 2016

REBELLION

Rebellion is as witchcraft,
so the good book says.
Why then must so many people do
just what they want instead?
The Bible says to obey them
who have rule over you,
but, when we don't, the chances are
we'll pay rebellion's due.

- Randy Boyd, 11-15-2015

A PROMISE BROKEN

A promise made
In good faith,
Or so I thought,
Later broken.
So be it, my dear.
Remember the day
When in the future
You reap what you have sewn.
So be it, my dear.

-Randy Boyd, October, 2015

BAGGAGE LOST

Years of sin, they took their toll,
Running from God quickly got old.
The baggage of sin dragged me down.
No smiles from me, always a frown.
Lost I was, no hope for me,
Hell is where I thought I'd be.
I didn't think I could be forgiven.
I never thought of going to heaven.
Until one day I met a man
Who began to tell me about God's plan.
He talked of hope and talked of love,
A Savior who came down from above,
God so loved the world that He gave his son,
From Him I will no longer run.
He loved me enough to die for me,
From all my baggage He set me free.
He saved me by His amazing grace.
I'm now secure in His embrace.
Jesus Christ is all to me.
One day with Him in heaven I'll be.

-Randy Boyd, March, 2016

Ramblings of an Old Guy — Randall L. Boyd

REFLECTING ON THE PAST

When I reflect on my past
I see my childhood and youth,
and I think of my parents and my brother.
Grandparents, aunts, uncles.
The good times were many.
Memories still there.

I remember the zoo,
days spent at Six Flags,
the vacations at the lake,
The Texas State Fair,
and fishing with my dad.
Memories still there.

Birthdays and Christmases,
Fourth of Julys, trips to the park,
road trips to see my grandparents,
and sleeping on grand mother's
screened in porch.
Memories still there.

My first day of school, and
each school year from first
through high school,
all the teachers, all the friends,
The good times were many.
Memories still there.

Football games, dances,
field trips, pep rallies,
basketball games, spirit week,
state championship game,
senior week, graduation,
Memories still there.

Ramblings of an Old Guy — Randall L. Boyd

I remember my first date,
I kissed her, yes I did!
Later lots of dates, lots of kisses,
with numerous girlfriends
along the way. Memories now,
Memories still there.

All can be enjoyed again,
as often as I wish.
Time after time
it all comes rushing back,
as if it were happening now.
Memories still there.

- Randy Boyd, 10-15-2015

COMINGS & GOINGS

'Round and 'round life goes,
life is full of comings and goings.
Happy times come,
they give way to sad times.
Sad times, sooner or later,
must yield to happiness again.
And so it goes, 'round and 'round.
It goes around, it comes around.
Such is life, full of comings and goings.

--Randy Boyd, April, 2003

SHE IS STRENGTH

She stands tall
In the face of adversity.
She shoulders a burden
No wife and mother
Should ever have to bear.
Two small children
Who she adores,
And they adore her.
They don't get to spend
As much time with her
As they would like.
She is gone all day,
Doing what she must do
To take care of them.
Life has dealt a harsh blow,
Yet she stands tall
In the face of adversity.
Her strength amazes me.

-Randy Boyd, March, 2016

INTRODUCING
OUR FIRST GUEST AUTHOR

CHRISTIE TAYLOR DUSCHEL

I met Christie in 1994 when she, along with her brother and sister, moved from Oklahoma to Tupelo, Mississippi, and started school at Tupelo Christian Academy, where I was on staff.

Christie was one of those students who just stood out. She was very creative and one of the most talented young artists I had ever met. The first time I saw one of her paintings it blew my mind – absolutely gorgeous. Christie quickly became friends with my kids, especially my daughter, Andrea, and we got to know her very well.

Christie, along with her husband and three children, live in the Lincolnton, North Carolina area, where she teaches school.

In addition to teaching school, Christie is a very innovative and creative artist. She conducts Nature Kids Camps, Books Alive Camps, and other children's camps during the summer months.

Christie has allowed me to include one of her poems, *If I Can Find the Time,* which she wrote in response to a challenge I issued to numerous people during National Poetry Month. I think it is a great piece, and I hope you enjoy it.

IF I CAN FIND THE TIME

Thank you
for thinking of me.
I would love
to accept,
but I just do not
have the time.
You see, I work —
12 hour days.
As soon as I get home
I have to cook dinner.
I have to get kids to bed.
I have a house to clean.
I fall asleep
as soon as I sit down.
I wish I had time
for some poetry and art.
OK, I'll try.
I'll see what I can do,
if I can just find the time.

-Christy Taylor Duschel
April 22, 2016

CHANGE DIRECTION

I walked along, watching
The menacing, grey storm clouds
As they thickened and turned ugly
As they darkened the sky.
Dark and stormy.
Gloomy and angry.
Lightning, thunder, rain.
Depressing.
A lot like my life
At one time...
I walked on.
As I turned the corner
And hurried along
I could see the light,
Breaking through the clouds
As if in victory!
Then I realized...
All I need to do
Is go a different way!
All I need to do
Is change direction
To see the light
And find victory!

-Randall L. Boyd, April, 2013

TRAVELING THE ROAD OF TIME

Time, it takes us down roads
we never intended to travel.
How time does change things.
But then, sometimes our plans
are not for us to make for ourselves.
The road is full of twists and turns,
when we travel the road of time.
How time does change things.

-Randy Boyd, January, 2016

WHY DID I FIGHT SO HARD?

I fought for you.
I fought hard.
I put my heart and soul
into the battle.
I look back and wonder...
Why did I fight for you?
Why couldn't I see?
Now I see clearly.
I was fighting to be humiliated.
I was fighting to be stepped on.
I was fighting to be lied to.
I was fighting to be cheated on.
I was fighting to be alone.
I was fighting to be ignored.
I was fighting to be treated like a dog.
I was fighting to be used for sex,
(When you aren't with someone else).
I was fighting to be hurt.
Hurt again and again.
Why did I fight for you?
I should have fought to get away.
I should have fought to let you go.
Now I am stuck with what I fought for.

-Randall L. Boyd, April, 1982

THE LIE

I found out the truth.
You lied to me.
I don't like lies.
Lies cause pain.
That lie hurt me.
The pain was made worse
Because of who you are.
You were raised better than that.

- Randy Boyd, October, 2015

THE CROWD CHOOSES

The crowd took Barabbas instead of Jesus.
So it is yet today.
So many choose something instead of Him.
Many choose money.
Some choose status.
Some choose material things.
For some it is fleshly desires,
Or drugs, or alcohol, or perversion.
Some choose pride.
They choose the pleasure of sin
Over the One who overcame sin.
Some choose a false god.
Some choose to worship a dead god
Instead of the one true God
Who rose from the dead.
Some care more about
What their peers might think.
They can have all that,
If that's what they want.
Take the whole mess...
Just give me Jesus!

-Randy Boyd, March, 2016

FEELING STUCK IN THE MIDDLE

I saw a turtle this morning
In the middle of the road,
Cars and trucks non-stop
Racing right on over him.
It seems he is stuck there,
In the middle of that road,
Too scared to move,
Not knowing what to do.
Sometimes I feel like that turtle,
In the middle of the chaos
Going on all around me,
Not sure if I should go on,
Not sure if I should turn back,
Feeling stuck in the middle.
Today I am that turtle.

Randall L. Boyd, May 14, 2016

DAUGHTERS

Daddies, take heed...
Take care of that little girl.
Cherish every little girl moment,
For time passes swiftly.
Soon she will no longer be little.
Now she is eager to hold your hand,
But the day is soon coming when
When she will be grown,
Gone from your nest.
Your hand she will no longer hold,
Though she will hold your heart forever.
So, cherish those little girl moments,
For soon that little girl will be gone,
Raising a family of her own.
Daughters are so special.

By Randall L. Boyd, May, 2016

THE BATTLE

Storms, they rage.
Darkness engulfs us.
In the midst of the storm,
Surrounded by darkness,
A battle rages.
The warrior faces obstacles
Daunting, seemingly insurmountable.
Negativity whispers to the warrior,
"Stop fighting, run, you cannot win.
You cannot overcome the storm.
You cannot fight in darkness.
Your battle is certainly lost."
The warrior, defiant and strong, says,
"Negative thoughts are not welcome here.
I fight with God.
He controls the storm,
Because He *IS* the storm.
He overcomes darkness,
Because He is the light.
I will not stop fighting.
With God I will win.
God owns the battle.
The victory is won."

Randall L. Boyd, May, 2016

SHE'S GOT THIS

Happiness was theirs.
They had it all.
Two beautiful children,
A house, a good income,
And she had started a business.
They were so happy,
Or so it appeared...
Or so she thought.
The perfect family.
And then... It happened,
Suddenly, like an earthquake.
"I don't love you anymore.
It's nothing you've done.
I just don't love you.
I want a divorce."
And with those words
Her world turned upside down.
Her heart was shattered.
The children don't understand what's wrong.
She does not understand.
She and her kids move out.
She cries as she walks away
From everything she had worked so hard for,
From everything they had built together.
She and the kids move to a cheap apartment,
With cheap discount furniture.
It's a place where she and her kids
Do not want to be.
Her kids say they want to go home,
But the apartment is home now.
"I must be strong.
I have to be strong.
I've got this. I can do this,"

Ramblings of an Old Guy — Randall L. Boyd

She says just before she breaks down.
Her kids have cried themselves to sleep.
She cries herself to sleep.
In the morning she wakes up
And puts on her happy face
And tries to be strong
As she gets her kids ready for school
And prepares to face the day.
She is strong.
She's got this.

Randy Boyd, April, 2016

WILL YOU BITE THE HAND THAT FEEDS?

How will you react today
when something doesn't go your way?
Will you speak kind words to those you meet
while you're walking on the street?
Will you be kind to those close to you today,
or will you angrily push them away?
Will you be angry when mistakes are made,
speaking words that belittle or degrade?
What kind of example do you want to be
to those around you, namely me?
Will you practice what you say you believe,
or will you bite the hand that feeds?

Anger is an awful thing,
it causes sadness, it causes pain.
So, how will you react today
when some little thing doesn't go your way?
You, my friend, are the only one
who determines your reaction when adversity comes.
Will you react with anger, will you yell and shout,
putting me down and cussing me out?
Tonight, my friend, when you go to bed
will you go regretting what you have said?
Did your reactions reflect what you say you believe,
or have you once again bitten the hand that feeds?

Randy Boyd, May, 2005

Ramblings of an Old Guy — Randall L. Boyd

FAILURE

There are those who think I'm a failure.
They think I am selfish, lazy, not worth much.
And those people would be correct
If thinking about material things and money.

For I have little to show for the years,
No property or fancy cars or wealth.
I don't own a big house, or even a small one.
There are those who think that's funny.

Friends and family have written me off.
I am old and life has passed me by
And I long for the days so long past
When life was good and days were sunny.

They don't understand what I do have.
I've stored it up in that place above.
I've tried to do good and to do God's work,
And my reward is sweeter than honey.

So think what you will, I don't care!
You're right, I have next to nothing.
I wish you could see what I have learned,
There is more to this life than money!

Randy Boyd, March 11, 2016

REGRETS

Be careful what you wish for,
because you just might get it.
Be careful what you throw away,
because you might regret it.

Be careful what you say in haste.
You cannot take it back.
Be careful who you turn away,
because they won't come back.

So many things we do and say
throughout the days we live
would save us so many regrets
if first some thought we'd give.

Randy Boyd, November, 2015

TALKS WITH GRANDMA

My grandma is so precious.
Her wisdom has withstood
time's test.
Long talks I have
With my grandma
Are absolutely the best.
I cherish these moments,
Because we never know
When one of our talks...
Could be our last.

Randall L. Boyd, May, 2016

Ramblings of an Old Guy — Randall L. Boyd

FORGIVENESS IS NOT EASY

To err is human,
to forgive, divine.
So it was written long ago.
A nice concept, yes –
but it isn't easy.
Seventy times seven times
is how often we are told
we should forgive,
that's what the Bible says.
Still, it is not easy.
Forgiveness cannot change
what was done in the past.
However, what it can do
is make better the future.
For us simple humans
Forgiveness isn't easy.
Inner peace we will never find
unless we learn to forgive.
What a dilemma this presents.
Forgiveness is necessary,
but it isn't easy.
To forgive or not to forgive,
that is the question.

-Randy Boyd, April, 2016

Ramblings of an Old Guy — Randall L. Boyd

THE NEVER ENDING CYCLE

To everything there is a season,
and a time to every purpose under the heaven:
Ecclesiastes 3:1 (KJV)

SPRING

At last, the winter has yielded.
The thaw has begun.
Daffodils, hyacinths, and crocus flowers bloom.
Life begins to return.
Leaves are born anew.
Grass becomes green again.
Crops to be planted.
In the garden, new plants go in the ground.
The birds have returned,
how I have missed their songs.
The cold has been pushed aside by warmth.
Once again the earth has renewed its life.
Baby birds and butterflies hatch.
Life is good,
and the best is yet to come.
Her job done yet again, spring yields, as always.

And God said, Let there be lights in the firmament of the heaven
to divide the day from the night;
and let them be for signs, and for seasons,
and for days, and years.
Genesis 1: 14 (KJV)

Ramblings of an Old Guy — Randall L. Boyd

SUMMER

Summer, in all its splendor, reigns supreme!
Warm weather has given way to hot.
Flowers grow. Trees are green, some bearing fruit.
Crops are in the ground, tomatoes are on the vine.
The earth brings forth her abundance.
Summer fun is in full swing.
Swimming, boating, baseball in the sun.
Long days, short nights.
Life is good.
We pause to celebrate our independence
and the freedom we hold so dear.
Walks by the lake, fish to be caught,
cooked over an open fire.
Young lovers walk on the beach,
hand in hand, they kiss by the water.
Children play outdoors, celebrating no school!
Enjoy it now, my dears, don't waste a minute of it,
for summer's time is limited, sigh….
Too quickly, summer fades away.

And He changeth the times and the seasons:
He removeth kings, and setteth up kings:
He giveth wisdom unto the wise,
and knowledge to them that know understanding.
Daniel 2:21 (KJV)

AUTUMN

Sadly, summer yields, as it must.
The hot weather fades, to warm, then cool.
Crops must be harvested, and fruit must be picked.
Humanity rushes to enjoy the last days outside without coats.
Leaves change from green to red,
yellow, orange, and brown,
and then they fall to the ground to be raked and burned.
The limbs become bare.
The wretched gumballs begin to fall from their branches.
The last tomatoes are picked from the vine.
No more peas to shell, corn to shuck, the last peppers are picked.
The flowers cease their blooming.
The grass stops growing, the green fades.
Squirrels furiously gather food,
for they know what is to come.
Halloween pumpkins, carved into faces,
children in costumes, parties, candy.
The crops in and stored away, we pause.
We give thanks for our blessings.
Family, fellowship, and a feast.
The frost comes, as the air turns cold.
The days grow short, and the time has come.
Autumn yields.

And he said unto them,
It is not for you to know the times or the seasons,
which the Father has put in his own power.
Acts 1:7 (KJV)

Ramblings of an Old Guy   Randall L. Boyd

WINTER

Autumn has gone away, winter reigns for its time.
The wind blows cold and cuts like a knife.
The leaves are gone, the grass does not grow.
There are no more flowers. The earth rests.
Snow falls, a little at first, then more, then much.
Snow and ice become the way of life.
Oh, how fortunate are those people
who live where there is little winter,
for they are spared the cold.
Christmas arrives, a time to celebrate the greatest gift.
Presents, time with loved ones, a feast.
Then another celebration,
for the old year departs and a new year is here.
Parties and revelry - and then... the morning after.
We give cards and gifts to friends and those we hold dear,
for they are, so we say, our valentines, so special.
The children build snowmen and ride their sleds.
Fun times, amid the bleakness of winter.
Easter season arrives, and
We celebrate the greatest victory, Our risen Savior!
Finally, mercifully, at long last,
winter's end arrives, and winter yields to spring,
and the never ending cycle begins anew.

Nevertheless he left not himself without witness,
in that he did good, and he gave us rain from heaven,
and fruitful seasons,
filling our hearts with food and gladness.
Acts 14:17 (KJV)

HAPPINESS

A new day dawns, bright and full of hope,
sunny and clear,
and then before the day is over, storm clouds come
and blot out the sun,
and the happiness is gone.

A new idea comes to a brilliant mind,
and it is a good idea, and you are full of happiness
because it is a good idea,
Then someone comes along and shoots it down,
and the happiness is gone.

A new life comes into the world, beautiful and innocent,
and everyone is happy.
The life grows and matures, and all seems well,
then something happens, and life is corrupted by evil,
and the happiness is gone.

A project is started, and you work so hard to bring it to fruition,
and finally you succeed, it is finished, your work is complete.
It is all that you expected, and you are happy.
Then someone destroys it,
and the happiness is gone.

Such is life. So we must start over.
And when we do,
happiness is born anew.

Randy Boyd, May, 2002

HOLDING UP TRAFFIC ON THE FREEWAY

This can't be happening.
I will wake up soon.
Come on, for God's sake,
it's raining like crazy out here.
Start, blast you!

This is a freeway you crappy old car.
It's 7:30 in the morning.
It's raining, I'm late, so
start, blast you!

Another one fingered gesture
from a driver of a new Mercedes.
Just what I needed.
Oh God, not a cop. WHY ME?
Start. PLEEEEEEEZ START!!!

I'm sorry, officer, I don't know what's wrong.
It just stalled. It won't start.
WHAT?! Get out of the car?
Officer, please, it's raining...

Standing beside my car. In the rain.
Getting wet. Very wet.
The officer starts my car.
Yes, I said he started my blasted car.
The officer says to pull the car over.

So I get in and start to pull it over.
It stalls again. Officer's face is getting red.
Now I am blocking TWO lanes.
On the freeway. I-35.
In Dallas. It's rush hour. It's raining.

Ramblings of an Old Guy — Randall L. Boyd

The officer calls for a tow truck.
WHAT?! A sobriety test?

It's early. I haven't even had time to get drunk.
WHAT?! A ticket? For What!!
I didn't mean for it to stop.
Why won't you START?

I hear a ringing noise in my ears.
Suddenly I'm in a fog.
I wake up.
It was a DREAM!

I look out the window.
It is raining like crazy.
I'm calling in sick.
No way I'm getting on I-35 today.
Not after what I just went through.

Randy Boyd, June, 1973

THE BOX

On a shelf in my closet, way up high,
Sat an old dusty box, long forgotten.
It was full of memories of days gone by,
Times that were good and some that were rotten.

After years on the shelf, gathering dust,
I discovered that box while cleaning.
After much thought, I decided I must
See if the contents still had any meaning.

So down came the box from that shelf way up high,
And I dusted it off and lifted the lid.
Much to my surprise, I just could not see why
I had valued these things at all, but I did.

So out went that box from so long ago.
Into the trash those unimportant things went.
How strange it was and surprising to know
After years had gone by, how little it meant.

Randy Boyd, January 20, 2016

WE MUST NOT FAIL

This is my house, let's make that clear.
I am the reason you are here.
Our rules will surely be obeyed.
I'm not your mom. I'm not your maid.
You have a room, so keep it clean.
Your dirty clothes will not be seen.
You'll keep them washed and keep them dried,
not thrown around and kicked aside.
When it's time to eat you will be there,
neatly dressed, and comb your hair.
What you're told to do, you'd better do,
'cause be assured, I'm watching you.
If you have a problem, come talk to me.
I will try to help, as you'll soon see.
If you're the problem, rest assured
we will get it corrected, and that's for sure.
On Sundays you know where we go.
Be ready on time, you're going also.
In school you'd better tow the line.
You must catch up, you're way behind.
I'm doing this just this one time,
because I love you, son of mine.
Let's get this right. We must not fail.
We don't want to see you back in jail.

Randy Boyd, March, 2016

TALL AND BEAUTIFUL

There she stands,
Tall and beautiful.
The sun shines
Through her golden hair and glistens.
She is older now, and wiser.
She considers things more carefully
Than she did in the wilder days
Of her youth.
Youthful mistakes taught her
Many harsh lessons,
Lessons she learned well.
Those lessons made her strong.
Now she has her life under control,
And she is happy.
Of her I am most proud.

Randy Boyd, March, 2016

I DON'T MISS YOU NOW

I missed you when you left,
but I don't miss you now.
I'm better now than ever
and much happier somehow.
Your stupid, silly foolishness
no longer gets me down.
You said you loved me, BUT...
chased other men in town.
Now I don't have to wonder where
you are when you're running around.
No, today I'm happy just because
you're not around here now!

-Randy Boyd, March, 1984

TO THE FOOL WHO THREW HER AWAY

To the fool who threw her out.
Thank you!
Thank you for wanting her
out of your life.
Thank you so very much
for giving me the opportunity.
The chance to love her.
The chance to make her happy.
The chance to cherish her.
Nurture her. Adore her.
Appreciate her. Respect her.
As strange as it may seem...
Thank you for hurting her so bad
she would never want you back.
Because now she is mine.
I am hers. We are one.
I will do what you could not.
I will love her.
I will take care of her.
I will show her love and affection,
And most of all, RESPECT,
At all times. Period.
So yes, thank you very much.

-Randy Boyd, April, 2016

Ramblings of an Old Guy   Randall L. Boyd

The only song lyrics I have ever written. I was asked to write it by a neighbor kid who had a small band. His mom was a hoarder. The song is about her. About a week later the band was no more, so these lyrics were never published, until now, that is.

JUNK, JUNK

Junk, junk, my life is junk,
floor to ceiling,
wall to wall,
it's junk, junk,
my life is junk,
my momma went mad and filled my life with junk!
She went to the sale,
bought all she could find!
Oh, my Lord,
she's lost her mind!
Brought it all home,
stored it in my room,
and now my life is full of all this
junk, junk,
my life is junk,
floor to ceiling,
wall to wall,
it's junk, junk,
my life is junk,
my momma went mad and filled my life with junk!
Daddy don't let her go,
don't let her go back!
She'll fill her pink Cadillac
with all the junk that she can find!
You know I've already lost my mind
from junk, junk,
my life is junk,
floor to ceiling,

Ramblings of an Old Guy   Randall L. Boyd

wall to wall,
it's junk, junk,
my life is junk,
my momma went mad and filled my life with junk!

-Randy Boyd, April, 1976

Ramblings of an Old Guy   Randall L. Boyd

April 19, 2003... After many months in non-poetic mode, I find a poem running through my head. I have no idea where it comes from or what inspired it, my life is actually good right now. This is a new style of writing for me; all very strange. But I learned a long time ago, when it comes to you, write it down. So here goes....

I STAND ALONE

Can anyone tell me
what's going on here?
Can anyone tell me
where everyone's gone?
Can anybody hear me,
is anybody out there?
I just looked around,
my friends are gone.

Can anybody hear me?
Can anybody hear me?
Is there anybody out there?
Where have you gone?
Can anybody hear me?
Is anybody out there?
Trouble's come my way,
and now you're gone.

Why have you left me?
I thought we were all friends.
Friends forever, so we said,
and now you're gone.
All my friends have left me.
each and every one,
I never would have left you,
but now you're gone!

Ramblings of an Old Guy — Randall L. Boyd

Can anybody hear me?
Can anybody hear me?
Isn't anybody out there,

Why am I alone?
Can anybody hear me?
Is anybody out there?
This just can't be happening!
Why have you gone?

Forsaken by my friends,
I stand alone.

--Randy Boyd, April 19, 2003

Ramblings of an Old Guy — Randall L. Boyd

MOM'S KITCHEN

There is no place like mom's kitchen.
Her food is oh-so-good. It's special.
Breakfasts fit for a king, with
eggs, bacon, hash browns, biscuits and gravy!
The delicious aroma fills the house.
She is known far and wide
for the delicacies she creates.
Holiday meals unforgettable,
or just a mid-afternoon snack,
Sunday dinners so divine,
all are so very good, so special.
Oh, how fortunate are those
whose mom's kitchen is busy,
because when mom cooks at home
there's love in her food.

Randall Boyd, November, 2015

TIRED

I'm so very, very tired.
I'm really tired of trying.
Tired of all the hurting.
Tired of all the crying.
Tired of all the pretending.
Tired of all the stupid yelling.
Tired of feeling really worthless.
Tired of all the lies you're telling.
Tired of always being tired.
I'm just plain tired.

Randall L. Boyd, April, 2016

SITTING IN DARKNESS

Sitting in darkness,
My head is ringing,
Far away somewhere
A voice is speaking,
I don't understand the words or meaning,
'cause toward madness I am careening.
My head, it throbs,
The pain is screaming,
I can't take more,
I hope I am dreaming.

-Randy Boyd, March, 2016

Ramblings of an Old Guy   Randall L. Boyd

INTRODUCING
OUR SECOND GUEST AUTHOR

MELISSA COOK

I became acquainted with Melissa Cook many years ago when she was living in Tupelo, Mississippi, and was a student at Tupelo Christian Academy, where I was a staff member.

Melissa immediately impressed me with how very smart and articulate she was. As we became more acquainted, I discovered she wrote poetry, and we became friends. That was many years ago, and I am happy to say I consider her to be not only a friend, but also a colleague whom I admire and respect. Quite frankly, she and her poetry are awesome.

Melissa and her two children currently live in the Sacramento, California area, where she has a successful career in the insurance industry.

I have included three poems authored by Melissa, and also a poem which we wrote together. I enjoyed working with Melissa on the poem we wrote together. She would write a line or two, then I would write a line or two, and so on. The result, I think, is a very good poem.

By the way, one of the poems in this book is about Melissa. Can you guess which one?

Ramblings of an Old Guy — Randall L. Boyd

PURPLE

Purple.
I love your agility
You move in degrees of subtlety
Bright like Byzantine
Mysterious as Deep Ruby
Laced in Chinese Violet
And Deep Tuscan Reds
You remind me of Fall.
Purple.
You cover me softly,
Like skin,
Smooth. Elegant.
ROYALTY.
When Poseidon beat vehemently upon my mood
Your soft, calm spectrums, dissipate the blues.
I resurface to dry land,
Refreshed.
I honor your hues with all changes of the earth.
Soft scarves swirled round' my neck to welcome autumn leaves
And winter's bite.
Flowers...intense and fragrant greet the birds through my window sill.
Spring showers beckon Akua to give her blessing once more.
Purple.
You are Mauli ola.
I rest in your peace.
Glimmer on down in my soul.
Leave your residue inside my heart.
Resurrect me again in the morning.

-Melissa Cook, 5-6-2016

Ramblings of an Old Guy — Randall L. Boyd

DRAWING A BLANK

I'm drawing a blank.
My think tank is depleted...
Just when I need it.
But there's always something happening
on this side of the tracks....
Just tired of writing about that.
I'll leave that to the nightly news...
They like to embellish.
I wanna write about the possibilities
of life beyond these dirty walls,
where crack pipes don't lay
scattered throughout.
I want to write about beautiful women
I see kissing their children
and teaching sons about
chivalry and independence...
but I'm drawing a blank.
Could it be I've seen too much
in my seventeen years?
Maybe if I close my eyes,
and sit in silence for a moment,
I can create the image of hope
I see in my dreams.
Since these streets are so empty...
I can't let my imagination
mirror that sadness.
Because one day...
this won't be my home.

-Melissa Cook March 22, 2016

PARENTING

Parenting is a journey,

Not for the faint of heart.

Ever learning and growing,

Parent and child alike.

-Melissa Cook, April 19, 2016

FEELING LONELY, FOOLISH, AND USED

I can't say I ever thought too much
About falling in love,
So when I fell, I fell hard,
And lay naked in the bed of emotions
Ripped open and exposed.
He had my heart at his disposal, and...

I let him in.
And that was something
I had never done before.
I had always kept any man
At arms length.
Because round these parts,
Men don't stay too long past a minute.
They leave as quietly as they come.

But he lingered,
Like he really loved me,
And the longer I let him stay,
The weaker my resistance became.
And then he began to caress me...
With invisible hands
Penetrating to the origin of old wounds,
He unearthed all the ugliness about me...
Shed light on all the corners and crevices
Of my journey and called me beautiful.

Nobody had ever said I was beautiful,
And at that moment
I would have given myself
Totally and completely,
Without hesitation or reservation,
To him.

Ramblings of an Old Guy — Randall L. Boyd

But fairy tales belong
In the pages of some teenager's diary
Or in the memories of a widowed lover...
Just not here,
Where men can't be seen
In the light of day.
Around these parts they exit
As quietly as they came.
And so it was with him.
In the morning he was gone.

So here I sit,
With my heart shattered
And my world turned upside down.
Yearning for him to return
And touch me again,
And tell me I am beautiful,
And make me feel good again...
Because right now
I feel nothing but lonely,
Foolish, and used.

By Melissa Cook and Randall L. Boyd
June 6, 2016

Ramblings of an Old Guy — Randall L. Boyd

PEONIES

In the spring
When life returns
To the garden
My peonies bloom
In all their splendiferous
Glory.

Their bright colors
Are a sight to behold.
Purple and pink,
Of every shade,
Bedazzling in their
brightness.

However, before long
Their beauty fades.
Colors are gone.
Too short is the length
Of the show when
Blooming.

I love peonies,
And I dislike them.
They are so beautiful.
They tease me so,
For soon they are
Gone.

Frustration is mine
For a whole year
Because I must wait
To see my peonies
Brilliant in their colors

Ramblings of an Old Guy — Randall L. Boyd

Again.

Peonies.
A love-hate battle
Between myself
And nature
That I can never
Win.

Randall Boyd, May, 2016

MY SAFE ROOM

There's a room in my heart
that no one can ever see.
It is locked and off limits
to everyone except me.
The room is my safe place,
and I hold the only key.
No one has been in for years,
and that's how I want it, you see.
A long, ancient time ago,
when I was young and carefree,
I let her in that special room,
because I was too young to see
she didn't want the right things,
and she would turn on me.
Then she left, suddenly gone,
and I was alone again, you see.
So nobody goes in now.
Sorry, that's the way it must be.
It is my safe room where I go
when I am afraid, you see,
and I lock myself in, so
nobody can get close to me.

--Randy Boyd, January, 2016

REALITY

Life.
Death.
Which is better?
Which is worse?
Pleasure.
Pain.
Which is better?
Which is worse?
Happiness.
Sadness.
Which is better?
Which is worse?
Reality.
Delusion.
Which is better?
Which is worse?
Life brings death.
There can be no death
without life.
Pleasure turns to pain.
Happiness turns to sadness.
Reality becomes delusion.
Is life reality or delusion?
Pain, pleasure, happiness, sadness,
passion, anger, love, hate,
are these reality or delusion?
Or is it all an illusion?
It all runs together in my mind.
I can't tell which is which anymore.
Am I alive? Am I dead?
Am I happy? Am I sad?
Do I feel pleasure?
Do I feel pain?

Ramblings of an Old Guy — Randall L. Boyd

Or is it all the same thing?
To be honest, I feel nothing.
Will there be a tomorrow?

I just do not care.
It must be an illusion.
Perhaps delusion.
Nothing this painful and full of sadness
could be reality.
I hope.

Randy Boyd, August, 1983

THOUGHTS LOCKED AWAY

Her thoughts, they elude her, they are far away.
She searches high and low but can't find them.
She doesn't know why they went away.
She needs them now, 'cause her mind has grown dim.

There was a time when her mind was quick,
and she always had something to say.
Now thoughts elude her, 'cause she's old and sick,
So chasing her thoughts occupies her day.

It's obvious, somehow, as the days quickly pass,
That the thoughts which she seeks are not gone.
They still are there, locked away, held tight and fast,
In the abyss of her mind, and she can't bring them home.

Randy Boyd, November, 2015

THE IMPORTANT GIFTS

The important gifts do not arrive on Santa's sleigh.
They are not in Santa's bag.
They are not wrapped up in shiny paper.
They are not found under the tree.
They can't be worn.
They can't be used.
They cannot be programmed
Or watched, or listened to.
They are not to be played with.
Understanding, peace, family, friends, and love,
These are the important gifts.
So many people miss Christmas
Because they do not understand.
So much time is devoted to the material gifts,
Which are unimportant,
And too little time devoted to the important gifts.
And the greatest gift, He's all but forgotten.
So many are left empty-hearted after Christmas.
When all the festivities are over.
All they are left with are the lesser gifts,
Plus the headaches and the bills that surely will come.
How I wish people could understand
The important gifts.
And how I wish they would remember
To celebrate the greatest gift.
For God so loved the world....

Randy Boyd, December, 2015

Ramblings of an Old Guy — Randall L. Boyd

I was recently challenged by a colleague to write a poem completely from the imagination, since I usually write about "real life" situations. This is the result of that effort. It is a total departure from the norm for me, a totally different style. Honestly, I was every bit as surprised as certain others were as to what came out of my imagination. Challenge answered!

DECAY

A flash of light awakens me.
The scent of burning flesh is overpowering.
I rise and open my door
And I am choked by the acrid smoke.
Everything is gone
Except for
Devastation.
Destruction.
Death.
They are everywhere.
Something is slithering on the ground
Coming toward me.
I turn to run
But it strikes before I can flee.
Its fangs sink deep into my brain
Until I cannot see
Or breathe.
I am falling
But I never hit the ground.
My flesh is crawling as if rotting, and
I find myself in a river of blood,
Yet I am walking.
Corpses are approaching me.
The sight and scent
Of rotting humanity
Consume me.

Ramblings of an Old Guy — Randall L. Boyd

I must resist.

I must flee.
This cannot happen to me.
But I have not the strength
To fight or run.
The rotting corpses carry me away.
I protest, but to no avail.
Somehow I know
I will spend the rest of my days
In a horrible, dark abyss,
Where light is not,
And suffering is,
Wherein reigns
Decay.

Randall L. Boyd, May, 2016

Ramblings of an Old Guy — Randall L. Boyd

NOW HE KNOWS HOW TO WIN

Hurt.
Rejection.
Heartbreak.
He had experienced all three
In his past, when he was little.

Smart.
Talented.
Athlete.
He was all of these.
His future was bright.

Tender Hearted.
Loving.
Thoughtful.
He was all of these,
Until he got older.

Rebellion.
Anger.
Bad Decisions.
The road he chose to take.
It would lead to his undoing.

Drugs.
Alcohol.
The wrong crowd.
He was in over his head,
But he could not see it.

Warnings.
Second chances.
Probation.

Ramblings of an Old Guy — Randall L. Boyd

He was given the chance to change his ways
But did not take it.

Trouble.
Arrested.
Prison.
He could have avoided it,
But his addictions would not let him.

Released.
Probation.
Decisions.
He chose to walk the right path,
But his demons and problems followed him.

A wife.
A son.
A daughter.
He was blessed with a family.
But still, he could not free himself.

A move.
Far away.
A new beginning.
A gamble. A fresh start.
A chance at a better life.

Sobriety.
A clear head.
A new perspective.
A better life with a new outlook,
On a road he can see clearly now.

Temptation.
Demons.

Ramblings of an Old Guy — Randall L. Boyd

Battles.
Still they pester him,
But now he can keep them at bay.

Hard work.
Family man.
Happiness.
He fights life's battles every day,
But now he knows how to win.

Randy Boyd, March 27, 2016

DISTURBED

It is disturbing how disturbed we get
About problems we cannot control.
If we were as disturbed
About things we can control
As we are about the things we can't,
We would probably do more
To change things in order to
Avoid the disturbances.

Randy Boyd, May 30, 2016

ON BEING A FOSTER PARENT

When you love children,
You want the best for them,
Even if that means
Not being with you.
You pour your heart
Into those little ones
Entrusted to your care,
Through no choice of their own.
You help them through times most difficult.
You cover and wrap them in prayer.
You shelter, protect, nurture.
You love them like your own.
They often become family.
Sometimes, however, you find
It is not to be long term.
Suddenly, they are gone,
Placed elsewhere by the system,
Perhaps returned home.
You water the seeds you planted
With tears and prayer.
This is the heart of being a foster parent.
Will they remember
What you tried to teach them?
Will they remember
How much you loved them?
Some will go on to do great things,
But you may never know it.
You rest in knowing you did your best
To make a bad situation better.
You must accept God's will for them,
Even though it hurts your heart so bad.
Such is the heart of a foster parent.
Randall L. Boyd, May 31, 2016

Ramblings of an Old Guy   Randall L. Boyd

CONFUSED

I am trying so hard
To process it all
In so short a time.
It is just too much
For my mind to understand.
But, how could I understand?
People are trying to help me,
But they have not a clue.
I do not believe anyone understands.
But, how could they?
How can I explain to them
What is going on in my own mind
When I cannot comprehend it myself?
Am I crazy?
Have I lost it?
Or, is this completely normal?
I'm so confused....

Randy Boyd, June 2, 2016

BLESSINGS ON YOU ALL

Well you've seen it.
You've read 'em all.
We hope you enjoyed reading our poems
As much as we enjoyed writing them.
We tried to put into words
The emotion, passion, humor, love, and thoughts
Experienced in life's situations.
We hope we have succeeded.
Thanks for reading.
Blessings on you all.

About the Author

Randall Boyd was born in Dallas, TX. He has lived in the Little Rock, AR area and Tupelo, MS and currently resides in Hazelwood (St. Louis) MO.

He retired in April 2015 at 63 years old. Randall worked in retail for 3 years, accounting for 10 years, purchasing 2 years, and food service management 28 years, while also being a professional wrestling announcer. He has also served as a nursing home chaplain/pastor (volunteer) for 26 years and is still serving in that capacity.

Randall has been married for 32 years to the love of his life, Jimmie Boyd.

1 son, John, Grenada, MS
2 kids (my grandkids), Isaak and Harley

4 daughters:
Michelle, Kansas City, Kansas

Andrea, Hazelwood, MO (Husband Craig)
2 kids (my grandkids) Ella and Parker

Melissa, Hazelwood, MO (Husband David)
2 kids (my grandkids) Wesley & Levi

Reannon, Merced, CA (Husband Ryan)
2 kids (my grandkids) Ryan & Rachel

Randall has been writing poetry for 50 years. This is his first book.

www.ingramcontent.com/pod-product-compliance
Lightning Source LLC
Chambersburg PA
CBHW032211040426
42449CB00005B/537